Songbirds

RoseAnna Lucarelli

Copyright © 2023 RoseAnna Lucarelli
All rights reserved
First Edition

NEWMAN SPRINGS PUBLISHING
320 Broad Street
Red Bank, NJ 07701

First originally published by Newman Springs Publishing 2023

ISBN 978-1-63881-662-1 (Paperback)
ISBN 978-1-63881-663-8 (Digital)

Printed in the United States of America

To my beloved parents, Maria Regina Lucarelli and Filippo Lucarelli. You gave me all I need to love, live, paint, write, and teach. Thank you for my life, proud heritage, and vision.

To our everlasting love,
Rosa

Contents

Poems..1
   Private Collection 3
   Mamma..4
   Mother's Love...5
   Mother's Touch..6
   Papa..7
   Papa's Blue Sweater 8
   Cherub 10
   My Christmas Child....................................11
   The Adopted Daughter 12
   One Love...13
   Love: Certain Bet...14
   My Valentine..15
   Wind Songs..16
   Fare Thee Well...17
   Beloved Stranger...18
   Flight Companions......................................19
   Windowsill...20
   Sun Sparrow...21
   Robin Red Breast...22
   The Photograph Album..............................23
   L'chaim..24
   Life and Death 25
   Enmeshed..26

Greed	27
Sweet Revenge	28
Erosion	29
Kindness	30
Redemption	31
Forgive	32
Barely	33
Equality	34
Find Me	35
Street Walker's Lament	36
Lamb of Gods	37
Happiness	39
Humelah Himalaya	40
Sir Barrymore	41
The Miser	42
The Lawyer and the Rapist	43
Blind Mice	44
A Somebody	45
Sunday School Children	46
Our Beastly Old Chair	47
Foster Puppy	48
Rao's Christmas Card	49
Tributes	51
Maria Regina Lucarelli	53
Filippo Lucarelli	57
Nonfiction	59
Our Heroine: My Dog Cheri	61
Saint Frances Cabrini, Night Visitor	64

Family Photographs..67
Acknowledgments 79
Credits 83
Paintings, Drawings, Photographs, and Screenplay........87

Article about the author 92
    "Expecting rejection but accepted by first publisher!",
    Len Lear, Features Editor, Chestnut Hill Local

POEMS

Private Collection

A treasured mine richly ored
Boasts a cache of diamonds and gold
Violet amethysts are secretly stored

Its map is known only to me
And the misty whispering sea
Delighting us in our quiet mystery

Proudly silent it shall be
Until time unseals a rare beauty
Opening portals for suns to see

Ice storms shall strengthen
My love's private collection
Until my weathered reflection
Invites hope's recollection

Bathing the treasures it holds,
The sea shall finally speak bold
Blessing all jewels unsold
And the mystery shall unfold

Mamma

Mamma embraced Responsibility

Gave it a name:

Me

Mother's Love

A mother's love has no bounds

Without an ending, without a plan

Kind beginnings herald a soft sound

Promising hope throughout the land

A mother's gift is never lost

Finding us in our secret hiding places

Embracing us when we need it most

Guiding our spirit in all our races

Kind beginnings herald a soft sound

In a love never lost and always found

Mother's Touch

Mother's silent eyes remember

Her baby's windswept curl

And greet us once and again

In a stranger's reflection

Yesterday's rose-colored notes

Silence the years gone by

Yet, crimson Christmas ribbons

Still wrap our soft sighs

Papa

Early last century

An orphaned boy could see

A distant dove

It lead him away

Asked him to stay

Gifted him love

Papa breathed life into an oboe

Played melodies no one may know

Except God above

Papa's Blue Sweater

After so many nights in a row

Papa got sick and had to go

A kind palm tree heard me weeping

and before a week had passed

Papa interrupted his eternal rest

to visit while I was sleeping

I saw a vision quite plainly near

and asked him, "Papa, are you here?"

He whispered, "Of course, my dear!"

He spoke with a gentle smile

and told me in his quiet way,

"I shall stay for a little while."

He had to catch the next ray

"Papa," I asked, "are you happy now?"

"Yes." He winked and took a final bow

As he ascended toward the morning sun,

a robin cried: "He has a blue sweater on!"

The curious palm tree heard me say,

"Mamma, Papa visited me last night

he was such a handsome sight,

wearing his sky blue sweater!"

Mamma winked at the laughing palm tree,

her Italian eyes cheered Papa was well

Wisely, she spoke, "My child, you see,

no one wears a sky blue sweater in hell!"

Cherub

Silent child you will be found

Touching promised rainbows

In sweet cotton clouds

Listening to lilacs

Standing purple and proud

Capturing tomorrow's lions

Without a sound

My Christmas Child

My Christmas child conceived with love
Sadly looks down from up above
Peeking through misty clouds
Safely covered in her shroud

Come to me, light angel mine,
My daily thoughts are your shrine

My beloved Christmas daughter
Eternally blessed with angels' water
Gifted with our Creator's light
Your candle shall always burn bright

Come to me, light angel mine,
My daily prayer is your shrine

Be it this day, or perhaps, another,
A treasured child will greet her mother
Bountiful gifts of love I shall present
Lost kisses and roses with heaven's scent
Peacefully sleeping until I arrive,
Rest in my heart with silent life

My Christmas child receives my love
And lights my path from up above

The Adopted Daughter

Barely out of the nesting womb,
A child silently waited in an empty room

Staring out the window with hopeful eyes
A gentle mother cried icy tears, unspoken sighs

A miracle happened one day:
Someone special walked her mother's way

A messenger in the form of a dove
Bestowed blessings, our guardian's love

Entered a man with a generous smile,
Determined to stay more than awhile

Mother's tears dried as her blessed daughter
Was anointed with joy's holy water

The protector held her small hand
Together they built grand castles of sand

Trinity wove a strong nest called home
On a foundation the found family has sown

They walked many roads a new family
Proud parents for the world to see

The adopted daughter kissed the white dove
And whispered "thank you" for an everlasting love

One Love

Our love was once

Just a baby's ounce

A moment's chance

Within a second's prance

Of life's dance

Not a journey's gallop

A child's belief in Aesop

A taste of warm wine

In a broken cup

Love: Certain Bet

Love

Will

Always

Be

Infinity's

Certain

Bet

My Valentine

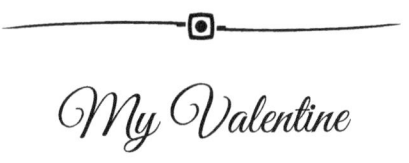

A blossom instead of a ring

Will accompany me to spring

Softly, I shall sing

Praises on my knees

For my king

Of trees

Wind Songs

Wind songs echo

In a room called home

Opening and closing

Yesterday's door

Until I beg them

To sing no more

Chanting to a burning hearth

Flirting with each flickering flame

Still asking me to praise your name

Timeless fires burning long

Kissed to life by warm wind songs

Force me to remember

I am alone with the embers

Fare Thee Well

Gladly, I will return

All fancies I hold dear

If you ask time to seduce

Me with its flirtation

And bid fond farewell

To a long winter's hibernation

Beloved Stranger

On your way

So fast today?

Your eyes locked mine

Infinity took its time

Your moment's glance

Raced a pony's prance

Our decisive feet

Spoke we shall never meet

Bittersweet

Flight Companions

Two wings harbored me elsewhere

Journey's flight companions

Escaped ordinary fare

A dove sent hope to transport me

To treasured gifts I longed to see

Fancy's flight through shuttered windows

Held my imagination ransom

Captured myself, a ceaseless foe

Until an ingénue arrived home

Windowsill

Weave your nest

On my windowsill

Leave me with your will

To nurture life

Love sees you at your best

And when your blessings arrive

Together, we shall rest,

My busy guest

Sun Sparrow

Bathing so publicly

In light's cleansing rays

Your piercing eyes

Held my lucky gaze

A second's sweet song

Nurtured hope strong

Your joyful flight

Is my sacred sunlight

Robin Red Breast

Proud robin's nest

Welcomes birth

Captures distant smiles

And fleeting mirth

Begs time to honor

Each blessing's worth

The Photograph Album

Once,

a passing fancy

of tomorrow's lost holiday

whispered a reflection

of my heart's desire

Once,

a prism's gentle ray

danced in an antique mirror

leading a silent spirit

to my soul's find

L'chaim

A lull and explosion

of mankind

A moment's repast

Silence

Circles fast

Life and Death

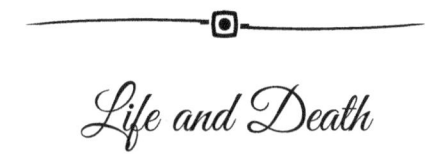

One week to create

A lifetime to experience

Sold in a moment

For half a six-pence

Enmeshed

Time   is the final sum
                    for humanity on the run

Hope   is the difference in life's equation
                    for children without a nation

Bound   by ashes and black circumstance
                    vision invited steel hope to dance

Spirit   draped in iron's willingness
                    shielded dreams from duress

Flesh   transcended temporal rape
                    as history encouraged evil's escape

Flight   heralded a lost generation to freedom
                    and welcomed anchors harbored home

Love   infinity's certain bet
                    wove freedom through the mesh of the net

Greed

When the bounty is right
        the mighty lose sight

Suddenly fair
        becomes unclear

The judicious eye
        changes its focus to I

No one shall heed
        it's simply greed

All flock with hasty retreat
        money has a great beat

The echo of an old piper's tune
        follow me, I'll take you to your ruin

Sweet Revenge

Seated at a crowded table,

a glutton is dreaming

of the sweetest confection:

the pie not eaten

Tempted by its sweetness,

savoring its delight

choking on a pit

impaled by the last bite

Erosion

Hatred erodes mankind

Caves a noble mind

Swallows flesh in quicksand

Delights a robber's hands

Kindness

Employ your Wise

Mind

To sow Justice

KIND

Redemption

Starve your affliction

and you

may

choke

your conviction

Forgive

Forget not an ounce

Forgive with abundance

Walk your path

With a merry dance

Silence your wrath

Barely

Barely, they listen

And cannot hear

Barely, they know you

And do not care

Yet, at your funeral

They will be oh, so blue

And Bare

Equality

Two and two are four
couldn't bore me anymore

Similarity and harmony
equal misery

Compatibility? Mister equality?
please, just bury me!

Companionship?
Mister Astute?
Not a fetching route
Count me out!

Joy is the difference in my equation
Shall I add another nation?

Find Me

Can't you see?

Find

me

Search near the sea

Find

me

Lose your key

Find

Me

Street Walker's Lament

Crossed many an

avenue

to find

YOU

Lamb of Gods

Once upon a new century

In a not so distant land

A microchip married a lamb

A cloned prodigy

Was meticulously seeded

Birthed into a world that created

Only what it scientifically needed

Intelligentsia jaunted the world

Inspecting brilliance

In all wooly curls

When this child became a man

He traveled stormy seas and distant lands

Alas, our brilliant prodigy

Could not determine his identity

He searched the world to find

A soul without a cloned mind

Desperately he longed to be alone

But everywhere our poor lamb went

Were Micro-Mary's baby clones

He became quite delirious

Echoing "Jesus, Jesus,

Everywhere I go there are always two of us

And am I really Micro-Mary's little lamb?"

Finally, one last plea

Up to heaven glanced our cloned prodigy

"My God, is it necessary

For the whole world to see

Another lamb just like me?"

Together, the Gods rejoined

"My sons, my sons,

Even We are no longer One!"

Happiness

Happiness is evolution's prodigy
Created by God's hands and our willing hearts

Our eyes see too clearly, shutting out pain's light
Winking at misery and adversity

Clever minds searching to disguise,
Offer little to broken spirits and bolted eyes

Humanity forges lies renamed universal truths:
When did it start? How will it end? Shall I arrive?

Yesterday's truths, pondered today, are swiftly disclaimed
And filed under tomorrow's lies

Search not paths soiled with malice, reach with your heart
Drink from your chalice

Happiness glances not with silent eyes, it travels secret trails
And echoes warm whispers

Awaken softly silent hearts, beat still no more
Happiness lives in your Creator's hands

Humelah Himalaya

Call me Jocasta,[1]
And I'll be twice baptized

On the wings of Mercury,
We shall soar to the sky

Burnt ashes rise from a bleeding urn
Yesterday's heart softly returns

A magician's charm covets me
Alone, is the place I cannot be

Oh, gentle magician, conjure me kind,
Unleash my spirit, silence my mind

Cast sand's shroud from a lost child,
Softly guide me on slow journeys wild

Fancy me away from a world of shrouds
Fate's flight escorts us through misty clouds

Away from a world where little is as it seems,
Our silent spirits soar a second's sunbeam
Kissing rainbows and finding lost dreams

---

[1] Euripedes wrote "They call me Jocasta…" in his play, Phoenissae, and William Shakespeare wrote "Call me love and I will be newly baptized…" in Romeo and Juliet.

Sir Barrymore

Caribbean skies splashed a pale hue
Once I met a man with eyes so blue
Hair as black as a raven
He is the talk of every maven
From Miami to New Haven
Of course, he is good looking and tall
The marathon's best runner of all
Yes, he is smart, adores the theatre and art
…mostly comedy, a little tragedy
Woe is me, woe is me!
If you ask me his name, I won't tell you
(Hint: It was printed in the New York Times
Which made him more sublime
Even though it was printed backward!)
Hush my mouth, did I say Edward?
All I can safely say today
Is he had such a charming way
Ladies and Gentlemen, 'tis better to stay
Out of charm's way
The dashing arbitrageur
Quickly traded mon coeur
Oh, dearest Sir Barrymore!

The Miser

Without a voice, his presence looms
Throughout dark and empty rooms
A mansion forged with another's toil
Chipped walls parade yesterday's soil
Mustard shades pulled down tight
Hinder life's light
One silent door chime never rings
A peasant's kitchen once fit for kings
Fare once prepared for a humble royal
Soured now in pots with nothing to boil
Dusty old diplomas still fatten his head
Poor wretched companion to the living dead
Trash scavenged newspapers carefully read
His singular daily ritual, life's empty mead
Not a chance left for fun and gift-giving
Laughter and presents are for the living
Mamma's and Papa's sunbeams are gone
To he who knows the price of all and value of none

The Lawyer and the Rapist

A tale of two sinners starts this way:

One day, a rapist entered the lawyer's lair
and paid a pittance for his crime.

The sullied swine snorted,
"Sorry for ruining a young girl's life.
Don't tell my wife!"

The cunning lawyer glanced at his books,
knowing just where to look,
to free his cronies and crooks.

"Kindred client," said he, "my library contains all that I need,
so, pay me with speed and you will be freed—
guaranteed!"

The rapist quickly departed
—had nothing more to say,
except, "Have a nice day!"

Naturally, the shrewd lawyer glanced the other way,
perennially pinching his pay.

On the Last Day, the swiftly sentenced swines scrambled into His office and paid for their crimes—perennially. Have a nice day!

Blind Mice

She entered the room

With the grace of a broom

Swiftly sweeping the air

Hurling soiled words unfair

Churning clear tides

Within her lair

And all were doomed

A Wagnerian souse—mouse

Birthed a toady louse

Together reside: a mouse and louse

Cloned in sterility's cold house

Evil always has its day

So, roll the dice thrice

Play until you make someone pay

Happy together, the wicked little mice

A Somebody

A sum-body

Is a nobody

With an addition:

Fiction

Sunday School Children

Boys and girls neatly dressed
Ravish a church school in their Sunday best
And help us celebrate a day of rest

Treasured dimpled darlings weekly appear
Eagerly listening to grand tales so dear
Dashing by with the speed of a mare

Laughing cherubs bustle and fuss
Secretly searching for baby Jesus

First, we whisper our names
And smile a big greeting
Then narrate tall tales
Since our last meeting

Teacher has something special to show
A shepherd and white candles that glow
A lesson is next about He who loves best
Followed by a reading from The Famous Text

With reverence we sing hymns and carols
Our proud cherub king chimes the bell
As the angels' procession marches through the hall

Our Beastly Old Chair

Together, is the best part of the day
As we share sweet moments of gentle play

Hugging and snuggling and laughing out loud
On our beastly old chair not proud

Just when I find a moment's time
Enter prancing pony paws that chime

Up, up, onto my lap you alight
And position yourself to snuggle just right

Knowing you are charming me
You lock your eyes until you can see

I have stopped caring about all things wise
While gazing into your Concord grape eyes

Don't worry, my little Mamma, you respond
Leave all the world's troubles to James Bond

I will gaze into your face so fair
As we snuggle together in our beastly old chair

I agree, my Valentino, you certainly win
We have so much fun—it must be a sin!

For Valentino, the most beautiful dog in the world!

Foster Puppy

Small puppy warm and cute

Please Sir, would you make your home hers?

"Adorable. No, the point is moot!"

"Oh, I love her so…but…
I gotta go!"

All jumps and kisses, sweet little Nanette

Looking for a friend, searching for a home

Everyone makes excuses…not yet.

Nanette, a mother you need

God sent me with speed

Our home is yours—

You will never be outdoors

Until another's love comes by

You shall not cry

Or, ask why

Rao's Christmas Card

T'was the week after Christmas
When all through the house
Pine needles were falling
Trembling our mouse

Crystal stars, garlands and holiday lace
Marched home to their perennial nesting place
Crimson poinsettias weeping pale
Trying to keep their season's regale

Spruce trees asleep on city streets
Huddled in an undignified retreat
When hark, I heard a sweet door chime,
A cheery greeting, this poem's rhyme!

Swiftly, I flew to open the door
Why, should I wait a minute more?
Could it be a postal delivery?
T'was the last Christmas card for me!
Pristine white as this morning's snow,
Rao's card made my heart glow

Resonant as a Venetian church bell's cheer,
Heralding joy and a jolly good year
The last Christmas card of the season
Keeps me faithful until next year

TRIBUTES

Maria Regina Lucarelli

Our Beloved Mother, Grandmother, and Great-Grandmother

ONE HUNDRED AND ONE YEARS AGO, Maria Regina was born on April 13, 1914 in Toritto, Italy, in the province of Puglia, a charming town bathed in brilliant light and soft Adriatic breezes. Mother married my father, Filippo Lucarelli, a handsome gentleman and conductor and music teacher, who was also from the same town, and had been educated in Rome. Their marriage in 1947 was sanctioned by Padre Pio, and blessed with three daughters, Rosa, Chiara and Agnes, and two grandchildren, Marissa and Erik, and two great-grandchildren, Avery and Sebastian.

MARIA'S LIFE WAS WHAT YOU MAY CALL A LIVING HISTORY. The stories of hardworking immigrants determined to survive and thrive in America, forged our paths throughout the years through blood, sweat and tears, and mostly hope, for the next generation. Her childhood in Italy was recounted with pride, and fond memories of a beautiful and bountiful land of olive and almond trees. And a youth of endless hard work: caring for younger siblings, chores, cooking, and sewing. My grandparents, the landed-gentry, inherited land and rented parcels to the contadini who farmed the land and paid whatever they could. The honor system was passed down to each generation. We were honored to own the land and twice honored to care for it. Mother inherited her love of our land from my grandfather, Pasquale, a hardworking farmer, and love of learning from my grandmother, Chiara, who recounted stories of our relatives who had emigrated to Argentina and became opera singers, lawyers and judges. However, in those days, boys went to college, as did my beloved Uncle Michael, who had learned five languages. Dutiful daughters were needed at home during the Great Depression, and Mother cared for her brother, Nicola, and sister, Lucia. An education was a luxury, not a necessity for girls, to be shelved and prayed for. God answered her prayer many years later. Mother always respected family values, and then it was time to return to Italy. A talented photographer captured her wondrous beauty and long-awaited departure in 1939.

MOTHER GLOBALIZED SELF-SUFFICIENCY WITHIN TWO CONTINENTS. If you could imagine a woman's hopeful face within Michelangelo's painting of God's hand reaching for Adam, it would be my mother's gaze with smiling eyes—arms outstretched reaching across the Atlantic. God helps those who help themselves: Always. Although Europe was devastated during World War II, thankfully, my family had all the necessities. They worked for it tirelessly. Once, Mother defied Mussolini, whom she believed did not have the right to tax the fruits of our family's labor. It belonged to our family, not a Fascist. That was that. Mother always saved for our family, with a strong hold on what was needed for the present and the future. "No" was not in her vocabulary. Mother made everything: always something new from something old. With a fashion designer's imagination and talent, her wedding dress, a gift from her sister, Lucille, was artfully redesigned into baptismal dresses for her daughters, Rosa and Chiara. An act of love without remorse or fanfare.

YEARS LATER, MOTHER PLANNED OUR JOURNEY TO AMERICA. Just prior to our voyage, we were informed that my father's papers were not in order. Undaunted, Mother boarded the ship alone and tearfully said goodbye to her heartbroken family. Determined, she left for America without looking back. Upon arrival in New York City, she worked day and night until she could furnish an apartment. She was a highly skilled dressmaker and assisted a fashion designer, Jonathan Logan, and made some of Judy Garland's clothes. One of her designs appeared on the cover of a magazine. After our arrival in New York, Mother worked at Saks Fifth Avenue and Bergdorf Goodman where her talent, skills, and hard work were recognized. Several years later, and with a new addition to our family, my sister, Agnes, my parents purchased a house. We moved to Long Island, and, once again, Mother and Father forged a better life for us. Our beautiful garden boasted of tomatoes the size of grapefruits and lovely fruit trees. Mother jarred tomatoes with basil and made homemade sauce, pasta, bread, focaccia, honey dipped carte-latte, and the best ricotta cheesecake in the world. And worked every day of her life until she retired.

MY PARENTS RETIRED IN FLORIDA. Mother loved Florida and visited New York every summer, maintaining her independence well into her 90's. She resided at the Brandywine Assisted Living residence in New York, where she enjoyed a lovely environment. At 101 years young Mother benefited from all the amenities and participated in a variety of activities, including exercise classes! She jumped hurdles and we have the pictures to prove it. Of course, she loved visits from her children, grandchildren, and great-grandchildren.

DEAREST MOTHER, we love you. We thank God that you have graced our lives. You have touched all our lives immeasurably. Babbo will take care of you for eternity. REST IN PEACE.

Filippo Lucarelli

Early in the 20th century, an orphaned boy left Toritto, a small town in southern Italy. Filippo traveled a long and difficult road and eventually arrived in Rome, where he knew no one. He found a resting place in someone's home and asked to stay; he stayed many years. He worked very hard and learned the skills of a fine barber. His new family taught him to prepare wonderful Italian dishes. He loved Rome and spent glorious afternoons visiting the Vatican.

Filippo was my father. He did not allow poverty to define him. He had dreams and worked laboriously to transform them to reality. He saved his meager salary and lovingly sent his tips to his aunts in Toritto. And paid for the education of a lifetime. He attended the Conservatory of Music at Santa Cecilia in Rome, where he learned music theory, and to play the piano, oboe, and accordion—just for fun.

One evening in occupied Rome, during the war of all wars, my father had to travel from the barbershop to the conservatory, and then return to his home before curfew. My father was captured and questioned by German soldiers. Fortunately, this incident occurred in front of a church. My dear father's angel helped him speak words of courage and wisdom. He humbly and faithfully asked the soldiers to allow one final prayer. They did, and the rest is my family's history.

The Nazi soldiers let him enter the church and an angel quickly guided him toward another exit, to a safe harbor called home. Throughout the years, my father's favorite Italian Thanksgiving tale was told: "The Nazi soldiers are still waiting for me!" Grandly, he toasted them with a glass of Chianti and beautiful smiling eyes, as my mother served traditional Italian and American specialties.

My father graduated from the conservatory of music and became a conductor. He had a marching band and wrote lovely music. His daughters and granddaughter inspired him. He named his heartfelt compositions: Rosa, Chiara, Agnese and Marissa. My father traveled throughout the countryside to instruct the farmers' children. Once, a farmer paid him with a fat rabbit. Filippo knew the farmer's dignified payment was far more valuable than all the money in the world. He accepted it graciously because he knew the value of the education he was providing.

My beloved father died on Columbus Day, knowing that I would remember him with a marching band and a tearful smile. The realization of our family's dreams—the impassioned dreams of Italian Americans, have graced and honored my father's memory with beauty and faith and creativity. And a proud parade.

NONFICTION

Our Heroine: My Dog Cheri

I went to an animal shelter many years ago hoping to adopt another wonderful dog. Cheri, formerly as known as Speck, a female Basenji-Jack Russell mix, charmed me with her circus-dog antics. Somehow, she balanced on her hind legs and fluttered her front paws in semaphore, without flying away.

I almost lost her to a nine year-old who had indicated interest just before I arrived. He had not claimed her, so I jumped right in because I knew no one could love her more. It was the beginning of another splendid relationship. All my dogs were adopted from a shelter in NYC.

Cheri entertained the neighborhood kids in Benet Park. They called her Circus Dog. While my cocker spaniel, Valentino, worked the senior crowd, hoping to find my mother among them, Cheri charmed the children. I must admit she wasn't always the easiest dog to get along with in the beginning. And it didn't matter. Our morning—before—work walks (Hello, 30 minutes!) resulted in returning home, where she would pee on the floor before you could say: "Late for work." And it didn't matter, when I found a shredded Manhattan phonebook scattered throughout the foyer. Looked like the aftermath of the Saint Paddy's Day parade.

Cheri loved Valentino very much and we were happy together. We traveled every summer, vacationing in fine pet friendly hotels and B and B's. My pets were always welcomed and complimented on their good behavior. I was told they were better behaved than the kids who had boarded excursion boats and trains. Naturally, I was a proud mom.

Then it happened one night: Cheri barked very strangely. Something about the sound of her bark alerted me. I did not attempt to quiet her or return to sleep. Moments later, I heard loud sounds outside my door. The building superintendent was banging on my neighbor's door, engulfed in thick smoke, as he forced it open. I immediately called 911, grabbed a robe and ran out with Cheri and Valentino. The police arrived within minutes. I unlocked the front lobby doors and pointed them in the right direction, asked if I could help them alert my neighbors. "Get the hell out of here!" was their wise response. Minutes later, you could not see your hand in front of your face.

We watched an expert team of police officers and firefighters evacuate the building and put out an electrical fire that had started in a vacant apartment next door to mine. My neighbors and I waited outside in the cold and in our parked cars throughout the endless night. We were comforted by firefighters who had provided blankets. When we were notified that we were no longer in danger and attempted to enter the building, I was informed that my apartment was not habitable. It was flooded. And condemned by Red Cross. Quickly, I collected a few personal belongings and Valentino, Cheri and I left our home.

I told the firefighters and police officers that Cheri had warned me. Thankfully, they told me no one had been injured. They called Cheri a "heroine," to which she responded with her usual circus-dog routine. Thank you, to the brave firefighters and police officers and Cheri for saving us.

Saint Frances Cabrini, Night Visitor

After undergoing a routine mammogram, I learned that further tests were required: I needed a biopsy ASAP. Frantically, I left the medical office, thinking the worst. I underwent an emotional upheaval and prayed more than usual, I confess. I negotiated with God, begging for a second chance to live. And promised: *A life would be saved.* Somehow, I would find a way to pay it forward. No questions asked.

I knew exactly how it would come to pass, after eliminating fostering, adopting, or kidnapping a kid. Since my promise was on fast-forward, fostering or adopting would take too long. *Think: Paperwork.* Fact: My cozy apartment accommodated all of my 5'2" self, a dog, and the mail. (Shoes don't count—always room for another pair.) It would be impossible, even for a growing imaginary kid. Anyway, kidnapping was mildly out of the question. Yes, only mildly, I was still thinking about the pros and cons: I fancied keeping the ransomed money for the munchkin's clothes and fancy private schools, and trips to FAO Schwartz. *No more shoes, God, I promise.* And art supplies for my students…

Being a catholic school teacher, my financial choices were always seeded by frugality. During our negotiations, I told HIM that I could learn to spend ransomed money as quickly as a winning lottery ticket. Throughout the years, I had taught thousands of students, so I figured: *I could really pay it forward big time.* Think again: *I would definitely be caught spending marked bills at the dollar store for my students' pencils and erasers.* Anyway, my dog, Valentino, would have to pay the ultimate price, as most pets of jailbirds often do. Besides, how many catholic school teachers have a history of kidnapping? (Please e-mail me, if they were successful.) God finally worked with me: *ADOPT ANOTHER DOG* pranced through my mind, as visions of prison food vamoosed.

Daily, throughout a month of living hell, I prayed to Saint Frances Cabrini. At night, I actually placed pictures of her on my breasts. Then one night, something strange happened: I saw a glorious vision of Saint Frances Cabrini's head, softly adorned in her traditional black and white habit. She did not speak, not even in Italian. Radiantly, she glanced at me, and had the good grace not to comment about her pictures on my breasts. I guess she obeyed her vows of silence in the afterlife too. The next morning, I wondered why only her head had appeared to me. The Italian women I knew were always completely clothed, and I might add, well-dressed from head to Gucci. But, I never questioned it. I was silent only because I was sleepy, and usually do not converse with visions.

Then, GREAT NEWS: I was fine. My peace of mind returned and it was time to pay it forward. I will never forget that snowy day as I marched to an animal shelter in NYC and adopted Buddy, a cocker-spaniel. Several days later, I learned that he had cancer. I notified the shelter, and was kindly offered another dog. I declined and kept him until… Buddy lived for several months. After we said our earthly goodbyes, I returned to the shelter and adopted Cheri, who has blessed my life.

Years later, I attended a conference at Saint Frances Cabrini Church and viewed a replica of Mother Cabrini enshrined in a glass tomb. The speaker mentioned that her preserved head rests in peace with other relics in Italy. I trembled as I recalled my vision of her gloriously adorned head. Her radiant eyes had locked mine and infinity took its time. My night visitor, Mother Cabrini, the patron saint of Italian American immigrants, had crossed the Atlantic Ocean, as I had when I was little girl, to protect and heal me.

Family Photographs

Maria Regina Lucarelli, my mother

Maria Regina Lucarelli is proudly wearing her lovely creations

Mom parades her lovely clothes and darling hat

My parents and me in Italy. Mom made our lovely garments.
Years later, mom made some of Judy Garland's clothes!

Mom is baking bread in our first house in America. I have never tasted better bread in my entire life.

My father, a graduate of the Conservatory of Music Santa Cecilia, Rome

Filippo Lucarelli and daughters, Rosa and Chiara

My parents, sister Chiara, and me in Italy

My father and me in NYC

Fond memories of my high school classmates
and bestie, Anita Karp Slavin.
Heartfelt thanks to Anita, Joan Fischer and
Bea Oertel for this lovely picture.

My father and me

Multimedia Preschool children and staff

United Way Campaign Fundraising Drive for the Mechanicsburg Learning Center publicized in The Patriot, Harrisburg, PA.

Dogs enjoying Central Park

Dogs enjoying the beach

Gracie with Santa

Marissa Ceglian Soran, Esq.   Erik LeRoy, M.S.

Marissa, my parents' granddaughter, sister Chiara's pride and joy, my beautiful and brilliant niece, received her undergraduate degree at Vassar and J.D. at Brooklyn Law School. Marissa, a distinguished speaker at the graduation day ceremony, discussed the importance of charitable giving, the senior class gift, and giving back to Vassar as I clearly remembered the day she took her first step in my home!

Erik, my parents' grandson, the apple of my sister Aggie's eye, and my nephew, a handsome young man of many talents, is an American College of Sports Medicine Certified Clinical Exercise Physiologist who received his Bachelor of Science at Cortland and Masters in Clinical Exercise Physiology at the University of Georgia. Erik competed as a Long Jumper at Cortland and is interested in music and astronomy.

Founding Faculty of Montserrat College of Art,
Beverly, Massachusetts, my beloved teachers.
Credit: Montserrat College of Art Archives.

Regina Lucarelli Family Photo Collage—Five Generations!

Drawing of RoseAnna created by a street artist

Acknowledgments

My Christmas child
The Regina and Lucarelli family
Old and New Friends
Kindness of strangers
Humanitarians
My students—one and mostly all!

My dogs Beaver, Rags, Valentino, Nanette, Allie, Buddy, Joey, Cheri, and Gracie
You are loved more than you may imagine.

My heartfelt gratitude to Len Lear, Features Editor, *Chestnut Hill Local*, who published my first poem, "Happiness," and tributes to my mother and father, Maria Regina Lucarelli and Filippo Lucarelli, and a story about my heroine dog, Cheri. You have honored my entire family and provided me with endless opportunities.

To Ms. Gwendolyn Davis, Senior Adult Librarian, New York Public Library, who read my original manuscript many years ago and firmly, unequivocally encouraged me to read my poems aloud to welcoming audiences in Manhattan and Chestnut Hill, Pennsylvania. You inspired me to pursue another passion: the joy of writing. Rest in peace dear, kind woman.

To Mr. Francis Chriss, stellar artist and dedicated teacher who demonstrated the proper way to arrange colors on my hopelessly disorganized palette and inspired my first poem long ago. Long after your death, we "met by chance" at the Philadelphia Museum of Art and celebrated the wonders of the circle of life. I felt a profound lifelong connection. Your presence engulfed me as I cried tears of joy, awestruck in front of your painting. Rest in peace, dear teacher and great artist.

To Monsignor Patrick Mc Cahill, Saint Elizabeth of Hungary Church, Saint Thomas More Church, New York City, my appreciation for the opportunity to restore the statue of Saint Anthony at Saint Elizabeth of Hungary Church. Your kind words and sound advice not to settle for anyone or anything strengthened my conviction.

To Mr. William Ruane, our school's guardian angel, thank you for providing all the teachers at Saint Paul School in East Harlem with your exceptionally generous gift which I used to upgrade my first thrift shop computer to a fancy model and complete my screenplay, *Rose Petals*.

To Sharon McKenna, Sacristan, Saint Elizabeth of Hungary Church, your dedication and commitment to Catholic values and support to those in need of assistance due to hardships, countless losses, illnesses, and injustices, I express my deepest appreciation and admiration. God bless you, dearest friend.

To the entire Newman Springs Publishing team, for your professionalism, enthusiasm, and support. Thank you for the opportunity to finally share my poems and tributes and stories and honor my family eternally.

My deepest appreciation for providing the memorable photograph of the Founding Faculty of Montserrat College of Art to Ms. Jo Broderick, Dean of College Relations, Montserrat College of Art and Ms. Olivia Lejeune, Executive Assistant to the President of Montserrat College of Art, Beverly, MA. Thank you for the memories that do not diminish with time.

My gratitude to my sister, Chiara Lucarelli Ceglian, for providing several lost family pictures. Your assistance in honoring our parents is appreciated.

To all the dedicated gallery and business proprietors, catholic schools and churches, Bucks County Ballet, animal rescue missions, police and fire departments of Doylestown, New Hope and Lambertville, New Jersey who have displayed my paintings, prints, posters, and cards, I thank you from here to eternity. I am humbled by your interest in my artwork and commitment to support Ukraine and honoring the victims of 9/11. God Bless You!

Credits

Group art shows

Simon and Maier, NYC
William Penn Museum, *Women in the Arts,* Harrisburg Patriot, PA
Gallery Doshi, PA
Montserrat School of Art, MA
SUNY Binghamton, NY

Literary credits and publications

Original Screenplay: *Rose Petals*
Poetry: *Songbirds*, Newman Springs Publishing
Poem: "Happiness," Chestnut Hill Local
Tributes: *Maria Regina Lucarelli* and *Filippo Lucarelli;* Chestnut Hill Local; Italian Tribune
Nonfiction: *Heroine Dog: My Dog Cheri*, Chestnut Hill Local
Story: *Saint Francis Cabrini, Night Visitor*, Newman Springs Publishing
Article about the author: "RoseAnna Lucarelli," Chestnut Hill Local, Len Lear, Features Editor; Newman Springs Publishing Website (Facebook)

Poetry readings (*by invitation)

*New York Public Library; *Barnes and Noble, NYC; Muse House, Chestnut Hill, PA

Art restoration

Statue of Saint Anthony, Saint Elizabeth of Hungary Church, Manhattan

Photographs and prints

Canal Frame—Crafts Gallery, Pennsylvania
Chapman Gallery, Pennsylvania
A&J Custom Picture Framing, Pennsylvania
Black-eyed Susan Style, Pennsylvania
New Life Art, Pennsylvania
RUTA Art Shop, Pennsylvania
Greer's Garden, Pennsylvania
The Paper Unicorn, Pennsylvania
A Mano Galleries at the Five & Dime, Pennsylvania
Circle of Life Veterinary Clinic, Pennsylvania
Our Lady of Mount Carmel, Pennsylvania
Mount Saint Joseph Academy, Pennsylvania
Saint Anne Ukrainian Church, Pennsylvania
Doylestown Fire Company, Pennsylvania
Advanced Dental Group, Pennsylvania
National Shrine of Our Lady of Czestochowa, Pennsylvania
The Larder, Pennsylvania
Tabora Farms, Pennsylvania

As You Like It Gallery, Pennsylvania

United Way Endowment Recipient

Fundraising Event: *Harrisburg Patriot*, PA

Scholarship

Italian; Trinity College, CT

Paintings, Drawings, Photographs, and Screenplay

Paintings

Songbirds, Pastel Painting
Mamma's Blue Dress, Oil Painting
Rosetta Mazurka, Tribute to Filippo Lucarelli, Acrylic Painting on Wooden Panel
Jazz Dancers, Mixed Media (Reference: Forza Malizia Dance Company, *Italian Tribune*)
Dancing Notes, Acrylic Painting
Player Piano, Acrylic on Wooden Panel
Pastorius Park, Chestnut Hill, Pennsylvania, Abstract Oil Painting
Pastorius Park, Chestnut Hill, Pennsylvania, Mixed Media
Annie's Song Abstraction, Oil Painting (Inspiration: *Annie's Song*, John Denver)
The Red Piano, Oil Painting
Unbroken, Portrait of Erik LeRoy, Mixed Media on Wooden Panel
Cherub and Mother, Oil Painting
Cherub and Mother Two, Oil Painting
Marissa At Montauk, Acrylic Painting
Woman in Black, Oil Painting on Wooden Oval

Ghost Ship, Acrylic Painting on Wooden Panel
Montpelier, Martinique, Mixed Media
Remembering 9/11, Oil Painting
Remembering 9/11, Poster
Red Barn, Oil Painting
The Road Not Taken, Oil Painting
The Red Fan, Oil Painting
The Kimono, Oil Painting
Rose Petal Chapeau, Oil Painting
Woman With a Blue Shawl, Oil Painting
Woman Sporting a Beret, Oil Painting
Portrait of Zulma Melendez, Oil Painting
Red Ballet Slippers, Oil Painting
Ballet Dancers, Tribute to the Russian Ballet, Oil Painting
Orchids, Mixed Media
Bluebird, Mixed Media on Fabric
Fifty Flowers, Mixed Media
One Rose, Oil Painting
Reclining Woman, Oil Painting
Woman, Acrylic Painting
Madonna One, Acrylic Painting on Wooden Panel
Madonna Two, Acrylic Painting on Wooden Panel
Madonna Three, Acrylic Painting
Three Sisters, Oil on Wooden Panel
Girl With a Pearl Earring, Oil Painting (Copy of painting by Johannes Vermeer)
Yellow and Friends, Acrylic Painting on Wooden Panel
La Madonna del Botticelli, Acrylic Painting (Reference: Boticelli bas relief sculpture)

Note: In addition to the above listed paintings, several oil paintings have been lost, stolen, or discarded due to damages.

Drawings

Butterfly, Tribute to Maria Regina Lucarelli, Mixed Media
Butterfly, Second Version, Mixed Media
Elderly Woman, Blue Wash Drawing
The Artist, Wash Drawing (Copy of *Self-Portrait,* Rembrandt)
Horses, Pencil Drawing (Copy of illustration: *The Red Pony,* John Steinbeck)
Flower, Pencil Drawing
Pensive Woman, Pencil Drawing
Woman, Gesture Pencil Drawing
Woman Posing, Gesture Pencil Drawing
Woman Playing the Piano, Pencil Drawing
Playing the Piano, Gesture Pencil Drawing
Violinist and Conductor, Pencil Drawing
Ballet Dancer, Pencil Drawing
Spanish Dancer, Pencil Drawing
Cellist, Conte Crayon Drawing
Mother and Child, Pencil Drawing (Reference: *Madonna and Child,* Raphael)
Pensive Woman, Pencil Drawing (Reference: Pablo Picasso)
Clarisse, Model, Montserrat School of Visual Art, Gesture Pencil Drawing
Clarisse, Model, Poster, Gesture Pencil Drawing
Clarice, Model, Pencil Drawing
Madonna Holding a Chalice, Pencil Drawing

Madonna and Child One, Pencil Drawing
Madonna and Child Two, Pencil Drawing
Madonna and Child Three, Pencil Drawing
Madonna and Child Four, Pencil Drawing of Our Lady of the Island statue, Manorville, NY
Man, Gesture Pencil Drawing
Man Two, Gesture Pencil Drawing
Woman, Gesture Pencil Drawing
Woman, Gesture Conte Crayon Drawing
Woman, Gesture Pencil Drawing
Little Dancer, Pencil Drawing
Woman, Pencil Drawing
Woman Drawing a Bird, Pencil Drawing
James Dean (Two Versions), Charcoal Drawing
Water Jugs, Pencil Drawing
Water Jug, Pencil Drawing
Baseball Player, Pencil Drawing
Portrait of a Woman, Pencil Drawing
Elderly Woman, Pencil Drawing
Portrait of a Man, Pencil Drawing
Pope John Paul, Photocopy of Charcoal Drawing
Portrait of My Dog Cheri, Mixed Media on Wooden Oval
Portrait of a Man, Pencil Drawing
Untitled, Photocopy of Oil Sketch

Photographs

Montpelier, Martinique
Cycle of Life Sunflowers, Chestnut Hill, Pennsylvania
Pastorius Park, Chestnut Hill, Pennsylvania

Trinity: Iconic Cross and Birds, Ocean Grove, New Jersey
Old Friends, Ocean Grove, New Jersey
Silent Moon, Philadelphia, Pennsylvania
Winter Shell, Long Island, New York
View of the Hudson River, Tarrytown, New York
Regina–Lucarelli Family Collage, Chestnut Hill, Pennsylvania

Original screenplay

Rose Petals

>Violators crowd the road to redemption—
>let us clear the path with rose petals
>and a great merlot! (RoseAnna Lucarelli)

Expecting rejection but accepted by first publisher!

By Len Lear, Chestnut Hill Local
Originally published Thursday, August 19, 2021

According to the latest ProQuest Bowker Report (an analysis tool and resource for librarians), nearly 1.7 million books were self-published in the U.S. last year, which is an incredible 264% increase in just five years, thanks to the ubiquitous availability of computer technology.

In my humble opinion, one of the most difficult things on earth is for an unknown, unpublished writer to have his/her book accepted by a traditional publisher. I would say the odds are about the same as the odds that I will be the Eagles' quarterback next year.

Therefore, former Chestnut Hill resident RoseAnna Lucarelli (now Doylestown) admits she was shocked when she "submitted my poetry book to a publisher, anticipating my first rejection, and surprisingly, it was accepted! Newman Springs Publishing emailed an agreement and will send a contract. My book, 'Songbirds,' will be sold on the Amazon and Barnes and Noble websites; the publisher will create a website for me, and I hope to include several of my paintings, including 'Pastorius Park,' painted when I lived in Chestnut Hill. I was told the book will be released late this year or very early next year." Newman Springs is a hybrid publisher based in Redbank, NJ.

RoseAnna,72, grew up in New York and taught in several Catholic schools there. She rented a small room in a residential hotel for women in Manhattan.

"It was unbearably small," she said, so I explored the city. I organized my life in a few small pieces of luggage. A suitcase served as my dresser, linen closet, medicine cabinet and desk. I learned to survive on very little because I only had $26 dollars in my wallet when my husband left. I was too proud to ask my parents for money after a 10-year marriage to an attorney. Prior to that, I was an art student and modeled in a life drawing class.

"I was humiliated to model nude in front of my classmates and teacher, but I did not know what else to do. Funny, no one in art school really cared because everyone attends life drawing classes. But you cannot imagine how I felt. Sometimes, I think that I have not recovered. I only modeled nude once, but that was enough humiliation for a lifetime."

Lucarelli moved from New York to Chestnut Hill in 2012 and lived here until 2014. She says she "loved the unique shops, the Joseph Borelli Art Gallery, Musehouse (where writers read from their works), Weavers Way and the Farmers Market behind the Chestnut Hill Hotel (now Market at the Fareway).

Lucarelli was an art educator and artist who was employed by the Archdiocese of New York and the Archdiocese of Philadelphia instructing students of all ages. She has participated in group exhibits in New York and Pennsylvania. Her writing credits include an original screenplay, "Rose Petals," and she has read her poetry at the New York Public Library, Barnes and Noble and Musehouse in Chestnut Hill. At one point she was director of the Mechanicsberg Learning Center in Carlisle, PA where her husband was a Legal Aid attorney.

RoseAnna is particularly proud of her late father, Filippo, because "he did not allow poverty to define him… He attended the Conservatory of Music at Santa Cecilia in Rome, where he learned music theory and to play the piano, oboe, and accordion. He became a conductor of a small town band and wrote lovely music.

"One evening in occupied Rome during World War II, my father was captured and questioned by German soldiers. Fortunately, this incident occurred in front of a church. My dear father's angel helped him speak words of courage and wisdom. He humbly asked the soldiers to allow one final prayer.

"The Nazi soldiers let him enter the church, and an angel quickly guided him toward another exit to a safe harbor called home. Throughout the years, my father's favorite Italian Thanksgiving tale was told: 'The Nazi soldiers are still waiting for me!' Grandly, he toasted them with a glass of Chianti and beautiful smiling eyes as my mother served traditional Italian and American specialties."

When asked what person in history she would have most liked to meet, Lucarelli said, "I wish I could have known Laura Ingalls Wilder. I loved her books, strength, courage, tenacity, sense of responsibility, self-sufficiency and family values."

The about-to-be published author is also a passionate dog lover. Over the years she has had dogs named Rags, Valentino, Nanette, Buddy, Joey, Cheri and Gracie. "I rescued Valentino from a killing shelter in New York City," she said. "He was the most beautiful cocker spaniel in the world. He even modeled for Ralph Lauren."

For more information: roseannagracie@gmail.com. Len Lear can be reached at lenlear@chestnuthilllocal.com

A talented artist as well as a published poet, RoseAnna's oil paintings have been extensively praised, as in this work, "The Road Not Taken." (Color image shown in article.)

About the Author

RoseAnna Lucarelli was born in Bari, Italy, and has lived in New York, Massachusetts, Florida, and New Jersey. She resides in Doylestown, Pennsylvania. A graduate of Harpur College, SUNY Binghamton and a Dean's List student, RoseAnna is an artist, writer, and former educator and investment representative.

"Throughout many years, I have pursued a lifelong love of art and obtained various credentials and graduate credits at Hunter College, School of Visual Arts, Art Students' League, Monserrat School of Art, Philadelphia Academy of The Fine Arts, Philadelphia Museum of Art, Philadelphia Federation of Teachers Workshops, and Moore College of Art and Design. My beloved teachers, Francis Chriss, George Gabin, Paul Scott, and Ethan Berry strengthened my conviction to develop artistic skills. Ms. Gwendolyn Davis, Senior Adult Librarian, encouraged me to read my poems at the New York Public Library and Barnes & Noble in Manhattan. I love painting, writing, musical theatre, classic films, museums, and cooking."

Her favorite destinations include Italy, Switzerland, Nova Scotia, Bermuda, Mexico, Manhattan, Philadelphia, New Hope, PA, Chestnut Hill, PA, Lambertville, NJ, Key West, the Caribbean, and visiting every pet-friendly beach imaginable with her beloved dogs.